Garden Your Growth

Alyssa Bell

BookLeaf Publishing

India | USA | UK

Garden Your Growth © 2024 Alyssa Bell

All rights reserved.

No part of this publication may be
reproduced, stored in a retrieval system, or
transmitted, in any form or by any means,
electronic, mechanical, photocopying,
recording or otherwise, without the prior
written permission of the presenters.

Alyssa Bell asserts the moral right to be
identified as author of this work.

Presentation by *BookLeaf Publishing*

Web: www.bookleafpub.com

E-mail: info@bookleafpub.com

ISBN: 9789363301887

First edition 2024

*To Grandma Marcie. For encouraging me to
never stop writing.*

*In loving memory of Peanut. The goodest boy
there ever was*

ACKNOWLEDGEMENT

I am blessed to have many people I'd like to thank. First off is Gwen, the therapist I've had since I was 15. She's gotten me through the worst of my eating disorder and depression. I wouldn't be here to tell my story if it wasn't for her.

A huge reason for the stability I've gained is from specialized trauma therapy. Sarah has been incredibly compassionate as I work through traumatic events and encourages me as I navigate the turbulence of recovery.

Next are my best friends, Elizabeth and Emma. They have stuck by my side since junior high. They've witnessed my evolution and loved me through my sickest years.
Elizabeth is the kind of friend who will surround you with love and never judgement. She is my safe place. Emma is my rock. She encourages me to be my best and together we have grown up into strong women. Her parents have become my bonus family and I couldn't imagine my life without them.

I got married in 2021 to a gentle, jovial, and loyal man. Corey would do anything for me - including be away from his wife for a month while I was at my most recent residential treatment facility. He balances me, accepts me as I am, and I am eternally lucky that he is my person.

Last but not least are my parents. Man have I put them through the wringer! Between the heartache and medical bills, they are the real heros of this story. My parents never gave up on me, even when I wanted to give up on myself. They set the example of how I should love myself and I am endlessly grateful for their support.

Also thank you to God, for my gift of writing and the gift of recovery.

PREFACE

Trigger warning: Allusions of self harm, suicidal ideation, and eating disorder behaviors

Enough

Searching through the shores for a purpose,
A promise of a life worth living.
Hoping all that I am is greater than all I am not.
Am I greater than my flaws?
Chasing love in every direction except my own.
An emptiness that others cannot fill.
Forever wishing I was more,
More than enough.

The mirror I gaze into tells me I have meaning.
Finally it shows me what's within
A heart so warm it melts the coldest of souls
A heart so worthy of its own love.
The mirror shatters because I am more.
More than my reflection.
Enough just as I am.

The scale that I once worshiped says to run,
Run straight to the freedom of believing,
Of knowing in my core I am enough.

Enough to shake the world with my soul's
passion.
Enough to love myself so vibrantly.
Enough to heal my wounds and help the broken.

I am enough for myself.

You are enough got each day placed before you.
You do enough to live with joy and ease.
You have enough inside you,
Now rest easy.
You are whole
And you are enough.

See no one else can teach you of your value.
Your worth can never falter, it is yours.
No need to pine for love since it's within you.
You are more than I can say,
You are enough.

Breathe in
I am valued.
Breathe out
I am worthy.
Breathe in
I am loved.
Breathe out
I am enough.

On the Border

Being Borderline is being on the border of
normalcy.
On the border of neurotic and psychotic, sick
and well.
It's the times when life is going smoothly that
I'm reminded what I have is a disease.
No amount of joy counteracts the demons in my
mind.
I smile,
I laugh, yet everyday I want to die.
Seeming to function, seemingly happy,
on the border of relapse with each thought.
Being Borderline is a never ending roller
coaster.
Whiplash from the mood swings,
nausea after an episode, fear when you realize
there's no brakes.
All you can do is muster moments of strength,
and hope it is enough to hold onto.
Being Borderline is feeling.
Never existing.
Never resting.
Absorbing every word like it's the gospel.
I am convinced that being Borderline is not the
same as being a person.

Silhouette

I'm beginning to see the silhouette of who I'd like to be, the shadow cast behind holds my past darkness.
I'm starting to catch her eyes as I fear the mirror. She pulls my fingers out of my throat and lays them to rest on my heart. She reflects compassion instead of judgement. An outline glowing in hope, no longer shrinking toward the grave.

I'm believing once again all pain has meaning. She whispers words of healing like my prophecy.

I can't wait to meet the person I'm becoming. I can't wait to love her gently and to thank her for surviving.

My Body the Scapegoat

5

How sad that my body has to suffer for the pain
of my heart.

Less of Me

I would like to be less of me
Not more of someone else.
A longing to exist without the heaviness.
I'll fold myself down into dantier pieces
Solely for you to digest.

I would like to be less of me and mean more to
everyone else.
My heart suffocates each person that I love.
Please mold me like clay into a person less
extreme.
Let me catch glances of endearment and not pity.

I would like to be a lighter burden and have
feelings less intense.
I hope I can exist in moderation.
Please bubble wrap my heart,
Shrink me down or else you'll drown,
I would like to be less and mean more.

The Demons I Once Called My Friends

I miss the comfort of being sick.
The safety that comes when you lose your
sanity.
I miss the countings of my ribs,
2 digits on the scale
I miss tearing my skin to release the pain
I miss the demons I once called my friends.
But even on these tearful nights,
I know there's danger in nostalgia.
And in reality I see,
That joy exists inside of me.

I hate my need for destruction,
Longing for silver lines to turn to red.
I hate the fat checks in the mirror,
The scale my extra limb.
I hate the tides of tears tattooed to my cheeks,
The smiles were then a rarity.
I hate the darkness that clouds my head,
The pills I wanted to take me.
But even on these tearful nights,
I see the danger inside loathing.
Finally I can now see
That no disorder defines me.

Heart of Gold

Your broken pieces rearranged with golden glue.
Spools of strength sewn into your soul, and
bound with the freedom of feeling.

These broken pieces free your heart for love to
flow so freely. A gift splintered from your past,
now capable of holding something new.

Your broken pieces make you art, resiliency's
mosaic. Only hearts of gold will thrive. Only
golden hearts can stay.

If Only She'd Listen

If I could tell her all the things she needs to hear,
I'd start with the warmth that radiates from her
heart. I'd say she grows blossoms from bruises
and that her tears glisten like stars. That she's
beautiful despite her wretched pain.
I would say her ink stained fingers mean more
than her striped wrists. That her too much has
always been enough. I'd remind her that life
won't always be blue, and that one day she'll
learn to smile too.

Vodka

Very quick it reels you in
One too many, black you'll see
Drown your sorrows
Kill all fears
And maybe you'll find happiness

Permission for a Treaty

They say the mind's a battlefield,
So does that mean it'll kill itself?
My fears feel like knives to the heart that I don't
have proper armor for.
If I am both the predator and the prey,
How can I ever feel peace within my walls of
skin?
I try to carve my way out,
But I never make it deep enough.

They say there's a war in my mind
And I say we must protest.
Raise the white flag of surrender.
Paint it yellow,
Like the stars that always find a way to shine in
darkness.
Paint it blue,
Like the eyes I look into
Not to drown in,
But to float.
Paint it black,
To disguise the demons that forever linger.
And once you've painted on your smile,
And forgiven your scars,
Surrender to the battlefield.

Not as a death, but as a dawn.

If I am both the victim and the attacker,
I know the path to victory.
I see her strength and her heart that she so
effortlessly gives away.
Keep some love, sweet warrior.
Bask not in your mess,
But in the message you're creating of resiliency.
As long as you stand, you survive.
As long as you breathe, you'll bloom.
As long as you hold on, you have hope.

Here is your permission for a treaty,
To gather your mind to fight for itself,
Not against itself.
You must be in your own side, brave soldier.
This is a war worth your weary.
This is your armistice.
This is your triumph.
The reward?
Anything your heart desires.
You deserve everything.

Mantra

May I accept myself for where I'm at in my
recovery.

Bask in Breathing

When I sit in sunshine,
I feel the rays smiling on me.
The water stills my mind with the winds of
serenity.
Nothing else matters when I am aware of the
nature around me.
Able to sit in my body and feel.
Different from the kind of feeling that traps me.
Experiencing life through my senses instead of
through rose colored glasses of depression.
It's less of a struggle to wake up each day.
A furry companion who purrs as I awaken.
Proof that my existence matters.
Things greater than my demons.
They tried to drown me, so I learned how to
breathe.

Circular Thoughts

I don't fully understand my brain.
How can one not comprehend the very thing that
they are?
If I'm not my thoughts, and I'm not my feelings,
and I'm not my body, then what's left?
Nothing.
If I am nothing, then why do I feel so heavy?
Why are my tears impossible to swim through,
and why does my very own mind want me dead?
It's tired.
I know it's tired because my mind is me, and I
am nothing, so I was never meant to be this
much.
Too much.
For so much goes on in my heart that rest never
can happen.
Engulfed with love and poisoned by pain, unable
to survive without dozens of pills to keep my
brain fighting, I'm tired.
My emotion's too strong for my skin to contain,
yet somehow these demons stay trapped.
How come I cry and those demons can float
when I'm grasping for are to survive?
Grasping onto anyone who stops.
Onto anyone who can resuscitate me.

No wonder I can never let go.
I cling to each and every piece of joy,
You're my lifeline.
I need help.
But there's nothing to save, I'm not living.
But maybe, just maybe,
A life with you would keep me alive.

Dear Younger Self

Your heart will be trampled.
You will passion be used.
The places you thought of as home bring
betrayal.
You will struggle to settle from fear of joy
fleeting,
You'll tiptoe on shards,
You'll be bruised.

One day you'll discover home is within you.
You are never without safety in yourself.
Not everyone will hurt you,
Not every chapter will end in tragedy,
And you will rise above it all.

I Am Not a Doormat

Please don't wipe your feet on me,
For I am not a doormat.
It seems with age I've softened,
Molded in order to please.
Fawning for your validation,
Chasing accepting,
And allowing stampedes.

It's time to rebuild,
Add strength to my core
And remember the worth that's within me.
So please don't wipe your feet on me,
I am tired of being a doormat.
Right this way,
There's a detour around
No stomping in my healing zone.

Perfect Insanity

Perfection is as close to insanity as ice is to
water - an inevitable, unending cycle.

Find A Smile (a song)

There's lessons I should teach myself
And every day I try
To touch my body soft and sweet
No more bloody thighs
But sometimes I think I'm too messy
Cause I'm never fine but

(Chorus)
Wanting to die
Doesn't make you less worthy of life
Sweet little child
Hope is hiding close soon you will find
Take some love and give it back
Unto your heart
Instead of attacks
Suicidal girls can find a smile

My therapist says lots of things
I know she's always right
Affirmate and meditate
Will help me ease me mind
But sometimes I think I'm too heavy
Cause I always cry

-Chorus-

Wanting to die
Doesn't make you less worthy of life
Sweet little child
Hope is hiding close soon you will find
Take some love and give it back
Unto your heart
Instead of attacks
Suicidal girls can find a smile

And every day is still a struggle
I question if I can do it all
But I still try to win this battle
Recovery's for everyone

-Modified Chorus-
Wanting to die
Doesn't make you less worthy of life
Sweet little child
Hope is hiding close soon you will find
Take some love and give it back
Unto your heart
Instead of attacks
{I always knew that I could
Find a smile}

Garden Your Growth

I wanted to decorate your soul with flowers
I ached for your heart to be lined in my love.
I dreamt each night with my head on cloud nine
that our souls were conjoined there as one.

My mind always fluttered right back to your
roots
Those roots pulled me far from the light.
Your leaves fell into my casket like rain
And drained all the hope from my heart.

I was left quite alone,
My petals all gone,
Given, rejected from him.
No wind in the air
No breeze from the shore
Slinece snapped all remains of my stems.

The eye of your storm caused destruction.
Frigid feelings and birds with no wings.
No more buds, only thorns on my soul.

Each cycle sheds light for next season
May this be a season of love.
More sun and less rain,

No more thieves of my soil
It is mine to break free through the snow.

Clouds part and give me more chances,
To seek and to heal what's been done.
Though sorigg no time produced not one
blossom,
Many seeds forged a path up ahead.

Keep your shell and they will for protection.
Open up far too soon and you'll die.
But with just the right sun,
All the soil for you,
The season will bring anew life.

Bees buzz in the breeze of redemption.
Sweet honey they drip out like gold.
No seed can become without cracked lines,
This time they sprout up with more ease.
See springtime can teach you these lessons,
Now attend to this pain and you'll grow.
Beware of the birds that chord childlike songs
Only listen to hymns of your soul.
Only garden in time with your growth.

www.ingramcontent.com/pod-product-compliance
Lightning Source LLC
LaVergne TN
LVHW041254200726

843507LV00013B/2956